Eternity
in the Mirror

by

Graham Ford

Copyright © 2020 by Green Sage Agency

Payperback ISBN: 978-1-952982-00-2

All rights reserved. No part in this book may be produced and transmitted in any form or by any means, electronic, or mechanical, including photocopying, recording, or by any information storage and retrieval system, without permission in writing from the copywrite owner.

The views expressed in this work are solely those of the author and do not necessarily reflect the views of the publisher hereby disclaims any responsibility for them.

Green Sage Agency
1-888-366-9989
inquiry@greensageagency.com

Acknowledgements

Some of the poems that appear in this book
Have been published in the *Mozzie and Focus magazine
Of New South Wales.*

Also by Graham Ford:

For Three Sins or Four
It's Confidential
True Hero Worship

I want to thank John Drake for his invaluable input

Peace

My Soul, there is a countrie
Far beyond the stars,
There stands a winged sentrie
All skilfull in the wars,
There above the noise, and the danger
Sweet peace sits crown'd with smiles,
And one born in a manger
Commands the beauteous files,
He is thy gracious friend,
And (O my Soul, awake!)
Did in pure love descend
To die here for thy sake,
If thou canst get but thither,
There grows the flowre of peace,
The rose that cannot wither,
Thy fortress, and thy ease;
Leave then thy foolish ranges;
For none can thee secure,
But one, who never changes,
Thy God, thy life, thy cure.

Henry Vaughan

Table of Contents

In Cana (When a Disciple met Jesus) 1
To Expound on a Day 4
Backpacker (Ring Home) 6
It's a Boy 7
A Good Talking Too 8
Jill (The Remnant) 10
A Map (Humble Service) 12
Griff: The Manager of a Café
On the West Australian Border 14
The Accused 17
K&S Freighters 18
An Abandoned Church 19
Norseman 20
Eternity in the Mirror
(On the Day I met My Soul) 22
Chastity 25
The Cloisters in Nedlands 26
A Table Top (In Bethlehem) 29
The Last Day 30
Samson and Delilah 32
Judith (A Present Day Hero) 35
In the World 38
The Buddha 39
The Stop Over 40
The Soup Patrol 41

In Cana (When a Disciple met Jesus)

How shall I stay my might?
How can I calm my heart?
The Trinity's Beloved presence
Stands so stoically in the porch light.
So still, He is a tempting figure
Dressed in white for my delight.

Such beauty is beyond all design.
The red cheeks of His warm smile
Goading me to stutter,
To step forward and to introduce myself,
To offer a haven for His hopes,
To welcome Jesus to our party.

Worldly wise,
I can only shrink from His purity.
Thrilled my mortal remains
Seek to rest in His bright gaze,
In the joyful brown of His eyes
That rightfully crown His erudite mind.

A worthy companion,
He is a compact partisan
With the strength of a carpenter.
Sturdily He is more than ready
To take advantage of His efficacy.
Jesus is in a league of His own.

I cannot disguise
The troubles of my heart.
Doggedly, throughout the night
I jostled with the competition
Vying for the devotions of His gaze
Who none could defy.

His warmth was that of a saviour.
His mind was that of a mature man.
In the depths of the sea
There is no greater receptacle
Than the soft embrace of His arms.
In my soul was the urge

To steal Jesus from His garden
Of sweet looks and holy life,
To take Him into my rough lodgings,
To make His thoughts dwell on me,
To let us play in a green meadow
In the thorns of a rose patch.

Such a prize is beyond my kind:
An oaf with the heart of ice
Bent on crime when the way is clear,
Lost in the sloth of sexual delight,
As the earth spun on its axis
The gathering came to an end.

His mother took Jesus home with pride,
Glad that her Son's enduring presence
Had ejected wisdom from my intellect,
Disrupting the stillness of my reason,
Giving love its first wild invitation,
Making me dream of a possible dalliance.

But my patience was a little thin.
Within a week I was undone,
Poetically startled by the romance.
No wondrous day passed
Without His smile blessing my sleep.
Tortuously impeded,

My discontent increased
To lead astray my intentions,
When, impossibly, on Sunday
My feet would pass by God's house;
My boldness would give me courage
To dream of His delightful grace:

Finding a place in my arms,
His eyes bright and serene,
His cherry lips always speaking,
His black hair long and untethered,
My face pressed into His cheek,
"Hi, sweet Jesus!"

To Expound on a Day

To Faye you can enthuse
In Mount Druitt all year
That a helicopter fell
To land on its iron feet
In the Centrelink car park.

Beside Lisa, gramps too
Stood at the bus station
Enthused to see a cop
Jostle with his ear phones
Then step onto the bitumen.

His duty was his task.
That he had landed badly
Was no belly flop to a Lot
Who, intensely curious
Was drawn to a vantage spot.

Gramps and Lisa were told,
It was delicately explained,
That an exquisite girl had died
In a pagan nation that night.
Jean was her Christian name.

Hurt tears were to flow.
Damned was the felon.
The cop helped her cause
By finding blood at the scene -
Tender evidence of the outrage.

Viciously stabbed they say -
In an epitaph on a mother's grave -
A victim of a passionate affray.
The sort of thing that is daily,
A lady's pain is unsettling.

Yet James, Sully and Deni too
Were at the bus stop also.
With a cheer and without fear
They were entertained today
By a helicopter in the car park.

Backpacker (Ring Home)

A tender, hearted eccentricity
To put one foot before the other,
To open your eyes and look,
A self-preservation quirk.

Surprise!Surprise!
Your foot touches the ground
On a new and a treasured path.
All of your nerves are tingling,
Your senses are fully alert
For the everlasting thrill,
For the joy found on new dirt.
A sense of hearing heightens
Your eyes search from left to right.
Your organism has moved
One step further in life -
A footfall for a brain to admire.

An enterprising man has two feet,
Two legs to progress and discover
A world that dismays his mother,
With a new adventure that pulls at the heart
And a pioneering spirit that conquers animosity.

It's a Boy

Destined to be virtuous,
Drawn to God's call,
He was born to succeed
With the joys of a protected life.
When, dressed only in a nappy
He stood for the first time,
An inquisitive baby,
And his exquisite, blue eyes
Looked up and smiled
As his periphery met that of his uncle,
A relative whose grin reflected
His trusty demonstration
Of a hard-won contemplation,

"Now that is a nephew."

The youngster's father laughed.
Regally seated at the dining table,
He could only encourage the struggle
Of a child who was strong,
Who could not be undone
By the injustices of life.
The serenity on his face
Excited the boy at his feet,
Who was urged to live -
Egged on to remember
The joy of a doting father,
The expression of an uncle,
The celebration of the smile on his face.

A Good Talking Too

He stood and seethed
Then disdained a clutter.
He was attired in white robes.
It was Christmas day.
We had arrived on time,
A repentant crowd.

Resolutely, fervently
He pursed his lips,
Displayed his wrath.
He angrily butted heads.
Acrimoniously he told us
With a daring voice,

"That we had got it all wrong!"

His belly bounced.
On his toes he was wobbling.

"You shall not sin!" He called.

On Christ's birthday,
He told it to us straight -
An old, Aussie man
Who bluntly speaking
Projected his authority
When he told us to stay still.

On a day when we celebrate a child,
It was for us to listen:
As we were told to be good,
Not to put our foot in our mouths,
To walk in the path of perfection,
To live a life a mystic should.

Jill (The Remnant)

The massive explosion was deadly.
The special victim, Jill, was hit hard.
There was no friendly warning,
Only a sudden, shocking bang.
Then at 9:47 there was nothing.

A prominent Christ was there.
In the darkness He was not enigmatic.
He was a sympathetic hand,
A peaceful touch that was so tangible
That, on the day, the detonation was forgotten.

Then, suddenly, Jill was lucid
To hear the wailing ambulance,
To watch the worried paramedic,
But there was no distracting pain
There was only a surreal calm.

The comforting hand of death
Had a voice so sincere,
"Come with me," he said.
"You do not want to live like this."
But, with determination, Jill gritted her teeth.

She was to live a celebrated life
Without solid legs to stand on
But her life was filled with possibility.
On TV she was to play creatively,
As she laughed freely in a cast of dozens.

The prayerful paramedic looked on.
Holding Jill's warm, delicate hand -
The loss of blood was a concern -
As she explored her mother's words
That asked if she would seek revenge.

But a sublime love came forth,
A gentle, over-powering force
In a high-spirited child of God
And forgiveness took hold of her soul
In a heart over-flowing with perfection.

A Map (Humble Service)

Exhilarated Sister Agatha arose
Awakening from her solitude's embrace
Fresh from a winter night's escape.
A thrill in her heart inspired
To clear her eyes of any stain,
A vitality steadied by reason's reign.

She threw on her robes;
She combed her hair with an elated twist,
Her skin aglow with her unblemished rouge,
Happy with her trim anatomy,
A working girl with a judicial integrity,
Ready to work in her convent's bakery.

A girl with a simple hope in God's unity
As she found her true destiny
With an early rise on a cold morning
To bless her sisters with her stability.
A soul that brought great joy
To all athletes who had a rough night.

With a rattle of cake tins
In an enterprise without terror
Heated by the smell of hot, fresh bread,
The baker gave Agatha an encouraging smile.
Her face pale from a long, night's trial,
Profusely she offered the nun a welcome hug.

A map for Agatha to plot her path in
Offering to God a vessel to admire.
Her deft love is a simple creed.

Without it her aim is dust
Open only to decay and want.
In her body a purpose had formed:

To adore the gentle dawn,
To pillar the sounds of bliss,
When the hands mould the bread,
To turn Agatha's intellect to her fate,
Designing a life that she can perfect,
Giving her enthused start its satisfaction.

A hymn formed in the thoughtful clarity,
The gentle pastures of her light,
The justice that prevails in her work,
To bring to life her favourite hopes -
A strategy to take in her prayerful recipe,
Offering to God all that she can achieve.

Impossibly, excitedly and at four,
She opened the doors to the sisters
To give the convent its first activity -
A bakery with an ample decorum,
A family's concern and productivity,
Their spirited part in a busy dwelling.

An enterprise with an eager face,
Designed to serve its early customers -
Women with healthy and disciplined bodies
Who had jobs in the convent's industry.
Who ably relished her enthusiasm
As they spoke gleefully, in delight,

Of their rapture at breakfast,
Giving Agatha's soul its nourishment,
Brilliantly warming her thoughts
To a willing companionship,
Inflaming her wide, radiant eyes
With a smile of friendly spirituality.

Griff: The Manager of a Café On the West Australian Border

An ordinary day,
Many miles from the melee
Where the eagle flies
And fearfully the rabbit hides,
On a plain of few inhabitants
Where no tree grows,
Where in your heart
You know there is a God.

It is a plain where you sow
With an early morning rise
And a twilight good night,
When Griff welcomes
The visitors who are many:
$60 for a sleep in bed,
$20 for a steak and chips,
They are thrown out at 10 a.m.

In a prickly heat
Griff says his prayers.
With his wife he holds up his head.
He is a man of God
Who has forsaken the city
And he asked volubly for guidance.
He demanded an acceptance
That our God approve of his choice.

Fixed to the wall
Of a well-trodden diner
Where men eat breakfast,
While they consider
A figurine installed
On the wall was the truth:
That the manager of this roadhouse
Was in love with the Blessed Virgin.

He was a man who had fled
The uproar in the west,
A man led by a vision of Mary.
Full of faith he had discovered
The worship of a mother,
A woman who did not abuse
Who gave him hope in his venture:
A lifetime of joy in his children.

Now his wife was a dear.
Her womb had produced
Sons who had some mirth -
They laughed and cried -
The apple of their father's eye.
As he worked in the kitchen,
His wife would be at play
Caring for two boys with his name.

There was the warmth in the air
Of an early morning -
A heat that gathered men
To a fire that leapt
In souls drawn to the desert -
Where they found Mary in heart,
In the very existence of their spirit,
To calmly live in her presence.

Griff came to the border
Drawn by the vision
One rejected by a malicious envy,
By the men who usurp their city
With loud cries of accusation
To chase from their state
The man who saw Mary
By the lonely roadhouse east of the calumny.

On a plain Griff had a refrain,
A psalm sung by his customers
Who, like him, praised the mother of God.
He included in his prayers
The presence of a 'roo in the evening
Which Griff had embraced
In a sea of silent salt bush
That buttressed the joys in his life.

THE ACCUSED

The priest stood and looked.
He could, if he would
Notice the man:
A dilapidated fan of Christ,
A rebel if he ever knew one,
Saying the prayer,
Saying that he did care,
For the royal road of the cross.

They had two different views.
Both were heady with the news.
One was passive.
The other was dismissive.
One was humble
And ready for the blows
While the other was prepared
To be the hand of God,
To be destructive,
While the other only knew Christ's touch.

Outside the wind blew.
The rain fell in a cold swathe
And it was harsh in church.
Disturbingly, for a moment
The carrying of the cross
Was intensely difficult
But it was no chore
For the one who is abused;
There was only the priest to eye the accused.

K&S Freighters

A pallet of Arnotts is unloaded.
One container reveals ten tonne of UDL.
Mark is trained to stack cartons without a swig,
To operate forklifts throughout the week.

Young Geoff is as wild as a bull.
Boxes swung as his epithets flew.
He is soon to give men a piece of his mind;
You had to be quick or he is unkind.

The boss is eager to stand and watch.
He chews gum rather than smoke on the job.
Throwing a tarpaulin over boxes of tissues,
He added his weight by tying down the ropes.

His Angela was a pay master stout.
She had a fiancé so she left us in no doubt.
If we had a query she would put us down fast,
For we were the slackest crew in these parts.

In church, on Sunday, I offer my heart.
A steady mind is all that I can claim.
I thanked God for my health and part,
Then asked Mary for another week again.

Now Gomer, he was a truck driver free.
On the road delivering mining equipment,
A Christian thought is repugnant and hilarious
So said his work mates to a clot, "Isn't it awful."

An Abandoned Church

The church was so blue.
It looked out onto a street,
A busy thorough fare
With traffic that hardly sees
The treat of having a church,
A house of God at its feet.

The glass doors were closed,
An empty building of the Lord,
Dismissed by the pagans
Who had no interest in admiring
The tall steeple's stained glass,
Or the pew's mighty order.

A sad church is broken,
To its foundations it bowed.
Its part in the community
Was ridiculed and jeered at
By the people who needed
A loving God most of all.

As the cars rushed by
The church began to sag,
Its sides weary from standing.
It was painfully unrecognized
As it demanded to be noticed
By the men to whom God was a friend.

Norseman

The hut is small.
Ramshackle and hollow,
It appeared nondescript,
Dead, off the empty street,
Morbidly covered in dust
As no place for a home.

Yet the tin shack -
A dwelling by a mine -
Caught the imagination
Of a lump of clay.
It was her pad
In it she had her spouse.

In a bush habitat
There is temptation.
Yet torrid passion found a date
In an amorous embrace
As a man and his wife
Toil to find companionship.

In a misshapen hut,
A house of secluded intimacy,
Their favourite rendezvous
In a desert sanctuary,
The good Christ is in their abode,
Deep in the hearts of both man and wife.

Quietly they pray together:

"With glad timing I wait
For what is to be,
For that which I will become.
Oh God of my restless spirit
Acknowledge my faith.
Do not let me be overcome."

Eternity in the Mirror
(On the Day I met My Soul)

Expertly pressure is little
From eternity, a boy in the mirror -
A reflection of my hardy self -
My soul that appears younger
Than my grey and chiselled exterior.
My voice is thick and prayerful

And there is markedly a case
To say that my soul is the romantic
That had successfully dodged me
Since I was a pimpled youth,
Not like the lady that had ruined me,
But the soul that might laud my path.

In the month of November,
When eternity purged winter,
Spring was in my soul's waltz.
I met him on Sydney harbour,
On the dock of heavy boulders,
Under the obelisks of a coat-hanger.

In a café's stained mirror
He wore my shirt and shorts.
He sipped coffee from a glass.
I approached him with a line,
One that was suited to his time,
One to keep charity in his mind.

One so domesticated
As I am when attracted
Falls to his knee unconditionally
To offer the love of redemption,
To find a seat at my soul's table
With words that are worthy

Of a man who might be stable
With a roof over my head,
A message to press,
A Holden at the door,
The maitre`d at my elbow,
All of which might impress

A sage wit unoppressed,
An undeclared warmth.
Brown hair fell into my soul's eyes,
Baby blues with waves inside,
Sweet lips that were bright,
Cheeks that were dangerous,

Wrinkles that loved his smile.
As we talked we grew closer
As a couple with no barrier
To a joy in our life,
A soul without animosity
Or a spirit that has no outcry.

With starlight beckoning,
A warm night quickening,
We walked along the foreshore
With God in our hearts seeking
To make love's work easy.
We talked of our hopes unachieved.

Now we had met, my soul and I,
With no down turned lips
Or mad, violence equipped,
We easily broke the silence
With terms that revealed us
To be a couple with amour.

Sin took second place
To flee from our embrace.
As a walk along the boat ramp
Has our hearts beating aloud
And, tenderly, my soul observed
That my arm tingled sadly.

Charm was in our abandonment.
Life was in our humanity.
Poverty was in eternity.
We shed the world that we know.
Together, my soul and I, we found a light.
A pity that the churches were closed tonight.

CHASTITY

A silent solitude
Found at the kitchen table
With bedlam held back
By arm and stillness,
Breath so calm and able
To be regular with each inhalation.
The thought of death,
As annoying as the drip
Of water into the kitchen sink,
Is a meditation on the passage
Of God and his entourage of angels -
Is he present in the quiet?
A lone voice speaking of His treasure,

"I saw her once, then twice -
A blond girl with a smile
So young she drew affection
Then dashed it by appearing to blur."

The Cloisters in Nedlands

The quiet in an immaculate house
Was a great victory for a ravaged soul.
(At night a stolen car roared).
Not in public the nun recited in bliss.

Unseen she sat behind a grill that lived,
Responding alertly. At mass she was a mystery.
She sang of a heart aflame, one that is
Compassionate for souls that turn to Him in retreat.

She was a nun who listened with concern,
Who dug deep to resonate with her sorrow.
Unfortunately man had little to defend,
But she never gave up, he does not comprehend.

A fact that was not lost on a hard working woman
Who was troubled and uncertainly wed,
She was anxious to see how the nuns lived.
Resolutely she gave herself.

She avidly offered her prayer
To forget the incomparable slouch and a lout,
A husband who could not understand
How a woman could withdraw,

"From a world that," he insisted, "had no flaw."

So provoked, she escaped her chores.
Unsatisfied by her lot, the wife wondered
What life was like in there.
Her solitude was resounding

As she was deliberating,
But she thought of her children,
Of her home and responsibilities,
So abashed her heart turned to their care.

Stoically dressed in bright light,
Christ the only man she had ever loved.
The nun was calm in her intentions,
Her soul enticed by no earthly sight.

Yet her heart leapt suddenly,
It did a jig,
A magnificent flutter,
As Abel came visiting one summer.

A spiritual man, it was said,
One whom God had chosen for repentance.
He sensed her meditative presence
Then turned to their treasure

To ask why she was apprehensive.
He was struck by her purity,
In the throes of mystic spirituality,
She had no time for a treacherous ghost.

"Are you alright, my dear?"
He asked with a troubled expression.

In his soul was the One who was tender,
This was her one, fruitful reminder
That Abel offered to humane Christianity
A magnificent, living flame of love.

In an ageless convent
(A Carmelite edifice) that is perfect
In the eye of the repentant,
All sin was tossed from the stair.

One that rose into a heavenly realm,
Where her apprehensions
Caused the aims of carnal men
To sink during spiritual warfare.

Adorned with a determined gain
To follow in Christ's footsteps,
To seek Him in His sanctuary,
She listened to His speech gladly.

In her mind's eye, in her heart's fire,
Unspoilt by worldly distraction,
The nun sought her Lord urgently,
For her fears were for her sisters.

A Table Top (In Bethlehem)

Sitting still on the donated table
Accumulated DVDs wait to be read.
They are plagued by none
But often gain more attention
Than the shrouded, nativity scene
Standing quietly in the corner -
A handsome, dusty sculpture
With the baby Jesus in its middle
Tenderly admired by Mary and Joseph,

"The journey across the Israeli border
Was quick and full of dread."

This hidden, wooden artifice
Painstakingly made on the West Bank
By Christians whose days are harsh,
It cost sixty-five American dollars
And it was solemnly purchased by a man
Who stood in the grotto of Mary
Praying to withstand the assault
Of a 24/7 brute and a whore.
The wood of the cherished figurine
Stands as a memento of Israel.
It was deliciously carved from the cedar,
From the tree that is grown in lots
Alongside blocks of prickly navels
To disarm and fill the ardent valleys
That encircle the mountains of Galilee
And highlight the ancient, hilltop towns.

THE LAST DAY

The desolate day was calamitous
But eternal silence was its reward.
The fatal sound of activity died
As the industry of man came to a close.
No longer did he bask in the explosive dawn.

But as the last man died fearfully,
The pain of anguish was in his soul.
In Sydney town he could not calm his mind
And there was a disaster in his heart;
Disappointment filled his heavy dreams.

He had existed desperately,
Living in lust with his family.
His doting children had grown
To live and die in much the same way.
His wisdom was his treasured mainstay.

The industry that he had built,
By devouring land for its wealth,
Had offered a last puff of smoke;
The turn of the last cog was still.
Now the good Lord could nurture the soil.

As promised the day of judgement was here
As the last excited child rebelled
Or, meekly repented, as the last man had done.
Incisively, Jesus was to have the final word
As the judge of man's foray into the world.

The last surviving Galahs sang.
The kangaroos hopped into the spinifex.
The scarred earth continued to breathe,
Supplying to creation its existence
As the warm sun offered joy to clay.

But a greedy man was judged today
When the last penitent died miserably.
Without fanfare, he was made to pay
For his ugly sins, both varied and unwise,
For the foot-print he had left behind.

Samson and Delilah

In a pitch black hat,
She tucked her hair in.
A harsh black, swept -
Cool with some street cred -
Graffiti crudely written above her head,
An independently, tagged wall.

On her own Delilah was unknown.
In the cold wind biting,
Dejected and miserable
As a rat out of the pack,
As dismal as the beholder,
When Samson sauntered over.

He offered to hold her.
He gave her his arm and sympathy.
He acted like a gentleman.
He was neither drunk nor high.
He was stone cold sober.
He knew what he was doing.

He was full of confidence.
He wanted her head on his breast.
He fully gave his courage a test.
He would not rest sedately
Until her love was his.
He confessed that his heart was in her hands.

He talked to Delilah best
With his hand on his ribs
As he told her of his days
When battle was the craze,
How he and Israel had won the day.
Now, winsomely, he is diverted

By the smell of her minted breath,
The tearful timber in her eye,
The clarity of her tidy thought,
Her clear, unwrinkled brow,
As their tender lips touched,
Her hair fell across his rough cheek.

When he felt despicable,
She would loudly call Samson
A mighty, army battalion
And, if a lively romance was missing,
He would tell her he was able.
She would pull him down,

Rosy cheek to cheek
With his excited face in her hair
And her meagre frame in his grasp.
Side by side, belly to belly,
Whispering sweet melodies,
They found solace in each other's arms.

The day drew its glorious breath
As his perfect dream grew dearer
But suddenly fiercely malicious,
Delilah's cold heart grew icy.
Samson did not abuse her,
An irredeemable bruiser,

But still he was a reject.
He could not persuade her
With reason, with no resemblance
To an amoeba she had washed off,
Her cheek was not to soften his breast;
Her cherished eyes were no longer his prize.

Dejected and unrespected,
He lost a heart that had no claim to his own.
He is now in a philistine jail
And, notoriously, he is without Delilah
While his long hair is cut and discarded
In a harsh act of betrayal.

She never gave him a reason
Other than it was her destiny.
She clearly had other men in mind.
Samson felt like a toe rag
The floor polisher unwanted.
In her hands he is the one who is despised.

Judith (A Present Day Hero)

The dusk was a deadly scene.
The ground was thick with blood.
Dogs scavenged amongst the dead
And the women of two armies wept
As Judith left the Israelite camp.

Garbed lavishly in a copious red -
A gorgeous colour to prevail
Against the god's of the Assyrians -
A brave and unarmed Judith
Entered her enemies fortifications.

She strode into the Assyrian camp
Into a harsh array of sceptical men
Who rested from the heat of battle
But a masterly tingling rose in her devoted flesh
As the ever-helpful Spirit of God lifted her soul.

A daunting Holofernes raged
Welcoming Judith with a clenched fist
But, surprisingly, his anger was soon persuaded
To be merciful with the attractive woman
When she trembled in his great presence.

"Oh mighty, lord," she cried humbly,
"I bring good tidings
Of how the disloyal Israelites
Can be thoroughly defeated
By your magnificent and daring army."

Her youthful eyes were liquid brown
And, temptingly, she was dressed
With a perfume that dazzled men
But clearly Judith was a maiden in distress
And, slyly, Holofernes held out his hand

To lead apart the raven haired beauty,
Allowing her to lean against his arm
While she told him of her ingenious plan:
How she was to live, contentedly, in his palace
Where king Nebuchnezzar ruled forever.

Unaware of Judith's subterfuge,
He warmed to her reassuring presence.
Thunderously he ordered a party to begin
And, without delay, he called for wine to drink
As she openly praised his impressiveness.

To the conquered and enslaved nations
The brutal Holofernes was a dangerous man.
Fiendishly the blood of his countless enemies
Was desolate and mixed into the rapacious dirt
But Judith was a woman who bowed before him.

His delirious party lasted into the night
Until his oblivious captains were led away
To sleep in beds of luxurious fur
While Judith was a docile guest
Who pondered God's awesome will.

Like any naïve man, Holofernes fell
On his soft bed; he slumbered, drunk
But like an angry wife with a gun in hand,
Judith took his own sword and she killed him.
With a mighty blow, she cut off his head.

In the hills, the men of the living God
Awakened to look on the devastation,
Certain that their numbers were diminished,
That the Assyrians would outnumber their best
But Judith arrived with hope in her eyes.

Positively, her glorious deeds resounded
As a punitive Judith returned home in victory
Triumphantly bearing the head of Holofernes
High on a spike to be abhorred,
Soundly dispatched as the vanquished.

IN THE WORLD

I.D. rose to observe the world,
His head not in the ground.
In fact, I.D. flew so high in a whirl,
Uncertain, for all the earth
Appeared alien to him,
As a jumble sale of people sworn in.

I.D. meditated on the Lord
As an individual who opened the door
To a world of people
Who openly clamoured for more.
Without love, their mode of operandi
Brought I.D. to his knees.

I.D. knew that love was near,
A dear to all who worshipped God.
Yet I.D. knew that life was not so good
To a people who needed to be heard,
Their motives given to selfishness,
An urge to rule over I.D.'s intellect.

THE BUDDHA

I had a vision in '85,
A total surprise
As all visions are.
It was of the Buddha -
Fat and squat, as mean as Bob.
It rose out of the darkness
As I kicked a table
Clean across the room.

(A coffee table, innocent
Of any crime in any form.)

So my vision captured a scene:
A young, angry man
Fighting desolation by any means,
Seeing the violent idol
For the first and only time -
A malicious looking Buddha
So fearful as to frighten,
More malevolent
Than any angry, young man.

Petrified, I opened my eyes
To find cover, to seek a refuge.
Terrified, I ran to a secure shelter,
The hope of a dark night,
Fearful of the Buddha - a no God,
A fat enraged blob in my mind.

THE STOP OVER

Cool and clear,
The pitcher of water brings no tears.
It stands alone waiting to be rejoiced
By a husband who has no voice
Until he has drunk deeply
Of the clean water.

The well has little to tell.
Not of the man who dug so deep
Or of the child who fell into its pit,
Not of the landscape's thankfulness.
The housewife can illicit no speech
Nor a crow encourage a shriek.

Pure as the ground,
The water gives the homeless no frown.
A traveller calls out with glee
While the innkeeper passes it out for a fee
Yet Christ's praise is zero
And the alcoholic gives it cheek.

The town has a gathering place.
From it a husband can only admit
That profane evil is at work.
Sad tidings for the break of day,
A drop of water in the foray,
It has its place in a gentle theology.

The Soup Patrol

They stepped out of the unlit park
Into the gaze of the probing street lights,
Anonymous figures of various climates
Wearing shirts of different markings.
Some wore hats that were wide and dusty
While others looked sinister in their beanies,
Mostly adults with desperate disguises
Always broke and often unsteady,
All hungry, all eager
To put something in their bellies.

There were about twenty,
Mostly men who slept in the shadows
Dejectedly standing in the public's moonlight
Finding time to contemplate the world of Socrates.
There was even the odd woman amongst them
As dejected as their companions,
Hoping for a cup of soup, a few slices of bread.

When we stepped out of the van to greet them,
Some were smiling as they called out
To let us know that they were glad to see us.
Those who had seen us before
Were pleased to see that we recognized them
The odd, new face looked grim;
Despondent they did not say anything.

As they gathered they did not hurry,
There was no disunity, they did not push or shove.
They did not fight or take any more than they would need.

www.ingramcontent.com/pod-product-compliance
Lightning Source LLC
Chambersburg PA
CBHW030202100526
44592CB00009B/402